123

MUSCLE CARS

MUSCLE CARS

Alain Chirinian

JULIAN ⊗ MESSNER

An Important Notice for the Reader

You are not allowed by law to operate a car or a motorcycle without a driver's license. The laws of your state or country will tell you how old you must be and what tests you must pass in order to get a license to drive. In the meantime, you can enjoy reading about cars or motorcycles in this book.

The information in this book is based on the author's research and information received from the manufacturers of some of the cars and motorcycles. The specifications for the cars and motorcycles are general and may not apply to every car or motorcycle and every model that appears in the book.

JULIAN MESSNER and colophon are trademarks of
Simon & Schuster, Inc.
Manufactured in the United States of America.

(Lib. ed.) 10 9 8 7 6 5 4 3 2 1
(Paper ed.) 10 9 8 7 6 5 4 3 2 1

Library of Congress Cataloging-in-Publication Data

Chirinian, Alain.
  Muscle cars / Alain Chirinian.
    p. cm. — (Tough wheels)
  Summary: Describes fourteen cars with lots of horsepower,
including the Plymouth Belvedere GTX, the 1968 Shelby Mustang GT500,
and the 89 Corvette.
  ISBN 0-671-68028-5 (lib. bdg.); ISBN 0-671-68033-1 (pbk.)
  1. Muscle cars—Juvenile literature. [1. Muscle cars.
2. Automobiles.] I. Title. II. Series: Chirinian, Alain. Tough
wheels.
TL147.C47 1989
629.2'222—dc19   88-38357
                                                                       CIP
                                                                        AC

Photo credits and acknowledgements
Pages 6, 9, 14 and 17, courtesy of Chevrolet Motor Division, General Motors Corp.
Pages 18 and 21 courtesy of Buick Motor Division, General Motors Corp.
Pages 10 and 13 courtesy of Saleen Autosport
Pages 22 and 25 courtesy of Oldsmobile Division, General Motors Corp.
Pages 26 courtesy of Pontiac Motor Division, General Motors Corp.
Pages 42, 54 and 58, courtesy of The Chrysler Historical Collection
Pages 29, 30, 33, 34, 37, 38, 41, 45, 46, 49, 50, 53, 57 and 61, by Paul
Zazarine/Musclecar Review

TABLE OF CONTENTS

5

1989 CHEVROLET CORVETTE

🎛️ **PERFORMANCE:**
Zero to 60 MPH: 5.5 seconds
1/4 Mile Acceleration: 14.9 seconds at 95 MPH
Maximum Speed: 155 MPH

SPECIFICATIONS

 **ENGINE:**

Type: V-8
Valve Gear: Overhead valves, pushrod operated
Displacement: 350 cubic inches
Compression Ratio: 9.5:1
Horsepower: 245 at 4000 RPM

CHASSIS:

Body/Frame: Fiberglass body, steel frame
Wheels: 17 × 9.5 inches front, 17 × 9.5 inches rear
Tires: 245/50VR-17 front, 255/50VR-17 rear
Brakes: Front and rear disc, anti-lock system
Front Suspension: Independent, A-arms
Rear Suspension: Independent, lateral and trailing
arms

7

A New Breed

"Muscle car" means one thing: good old American horsepower! A huge engine with massive amounts of horsepower made rockets out of ordinary family cars in the 1960s and 70s. Today, some cars use new technology to carry on the tradition. Just a few years ago, many people thought that the Corvette had become only a shadow of what it was in the '60s and '70s—a car that had a beautiful fiberglass body, but couldn't generate horsepower like it did in the good old days. In 1984, all that changed. A new, better-than-ever Corvette was born.

Better Every Year

With each year since its introduction, the new Corvette has been improved. Horsepower of the 350-cubic-inch engine has grown to 245. Wheels and tires were increased to 17 inches. And an advanced anti-lock brake system makes the Corvette one of the best-stopping cars you can buy.

Under the Hood

To open the hood of the Corvette, you flip the whole front section of the body forward, just like on a race car. The beautiful aluminum intake manifolds curl around the top of the engine. Some of the rear suspension pieces are made of fiberglass too!

Success in Racing

The Corvette has beaten all challengers on the racetrack, from Porsches to BMWs. The Corvettes were winning so many races, it was finally decided that they had to race in their own class! Now, these Corvettes race only with each other, because the other cars couldn't catch up with the newest and best muscle car from Chevrolet.

1989 SALEEN MUSTANG

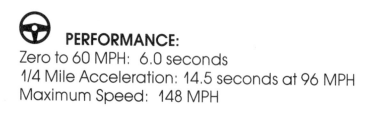 **PERFORMANCE:**
Zero to 60 MPH: 6.0 seconds
1/4 Mile Acceleration: 14.5 seconds at 96 MPH
Maximum Speed: 148 MPH

10

SPECIFICATIONS

 **ENGINE:**

Type: V-8
Valve Gear: Overhead valves, pushrod operated
Displacement: 302 cubic inches
Compression Ratio: 9.2:1
Horsepower: 225 at 4200 RPM

CHASSIS:

Body/Frame: Steel body and frame
Wheels: 16 × 7 inches front, 16 × 8 inches rear
Tires: 225/50VR-16 front, 225/50VR-16 rear
Brakes: Front and rear discs
Front Suspension: Independent, MacPherson struts
Rear Suspension: Live axle, "quadra shock"

A New Race for Power

In the late 1970s, most American auto companies stopped making muscle cars. By 1981, it seemed that the good old days of American V-8 power were gone forever. Suddenly, in 1982, the dreams of all Mustang fans came true. Ford offered a 160-horsepower V-8 with a four-speed in the new Mustang GT, and the new race for horsepower had begun!

The Best Mustang Ever

Ford continued to take the lead in the horsepower race by offering improvements to the Mustang each year. In 1989 trim, the Mustang can be had with a V-8 engine with 225 horsepower. The rear suspension has four shock absorbers, called "quadra shock." Having four shocks in the rear helps keep the brutal power of the Mustang under control when cornering and accelerating.

An Even Hotter Mustang

Today, the Saleen Autosport Company makes one of the hottest cars on the road even better. Saleen Autosport takes a Ford Mustang and modifies it with special equipment. To keep the Mustang's horsepower under better control, the front and rear suspensions get high-performance shock absorbers and other modifications. And best of all, disc brakes are added at the rear wheels for ultimate stopping power.

In the Cockpit

Sitting in the Saleen Mustang makes you feel comfortable about driving this car at high speeds. Its adjustable seat keeps you in place during cornering around mountain roads. The five-speed transmission shifts smoothly, allowing you to pay attention to your speed. The torque of this 302-cubic-inch V-8 pins you back in your seat each time you press the accelerator. If you press on all the way in fifth gear, you can reach up to 148 miles per hour!

1989 CHEVROLET CAMARO IROC-Z

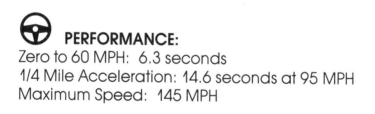 **PERFORMANCE:**
Zero to 60 MPH: 6.3 seconds
1/4 Mile Acceleration: 14.6 seconds at 95 MPH
Maximum Speed: 145 MPH

SPECIFICATIONS

 **ENGINE:**

Type: V-8
Valve Gear: Overhead valves, pushrod operated
Displacement: 350 cubic inches
Compression Ratio: 9.0:1
Horsepower: 225 at 4400 RPM

CHASSIS:

Body/Frame: Steel body and frame
Wheels: 16 × 8 inches front, 16 × 8 inches rear
Tires: 245/50VR-16 front, 245/50VR-16 rear
Brakes: Front and rear discs
Front Suspension: Independent, MacPherson struts
Rear Suspension: Solid axle

Modern Muscle Car

The IROC-Z Camaro gets its name from racing. The initials stand for *I*nternational *R*ace *O*f *C*hampions, which reminds drivers that this Camaro is a pure-bred champion. It is a modern muscle car, with a huge V-8 engine but modern styling. It has incredible horse-power but gets decent gas mileage. The newest Camaro is a car that anyone would love to have.

Like a Jet Fighter

Climb inside the cockpit of the IROC-Z, and you'll see a row of instruments in front of you, telling you all important information that you need to know. Just like a fighter plane, the controls are easily operated during high-speed runs. You sit low in the seat, and the long hood lies in front of you. Under that hood lies the mighty V-8 of the Camaro IROC-Z.

Sleek Styling

The sleek styling of the Camaro IROC-Z isn't just for looks. It has a shape that helps cut through the air. That is an important part of modern car design, and the engineers at Chevrolet did a great job. The form of the IROC helps it reach a top speed of nearly 150 miles per hour, and get good gas mileage. Of course, you can't do both at the same time!

Available Corvette Power

If you check the right option box of the IROC-Z, you can have it with a monster 350-cubic-inch engine. This is basically the same engine that powers the Corvette, so you know that it means business!

Racing Against the Wind

The road in front of you looks inviting. Curves dive up and down the mountain and you follow them closely in the IROC. Punch the accelerator, and you feel the massive tires take a bite out of the blacktop. Slow down with the big disc brakes, then you power "on" all the way. You're racing against the road aboard the Camaro IROC-Z!

17

1987 BUICK GNX

 **PERFORMANCE:**
Zero to 60 MPH: 5.0 seconds
1/4 Mile Acceleration: 13.3 seconds at 104 MPH
Maximum Speed: 125 MPH

SPECIFICATIONS

ENGINE:

Type: V-6, turbocharged
Valve Gear: Overhead valves, pushrod operated
Displacement: 231 cubic inches
Compression Ratio: 8.0:1
Horsepower: 300 at 4400 RPM

CHASSIS:

Body/Frame: Steel body and frame
Wheels: 16-inch, front and rear
Tires: 245/50VR-16 front, 255/50VR-16 rear
Brakes: Front disc, rear drum
Front Suspension: Independent, upper and lower
control arms
Rear Suspension: Solid axle, anti-roll bar

Limited Edition

When Buick decided that its Regal model was going to be redesigned in 1988, they chose to let the hot-selling car go out with a bang. And what better bang than dropping a 300-horsepower, turbo-charged V-6 under the hood? Only 500 lucky owners would ever find out.

300 Horsepower

The numbers tell it all: the GNX, with its 300 horses, can achieve quarter-mile times under 13.5 seconds. This car is so fast that the FBI wanted to buy some for high-speed chase vehicles. But there weren't enough to go around, so they settled for the Buick Grand National, the slightly-less-powerful cousin of the GNX.

Turbocharged Engine

The V-6 engine in the GNX is highly modified to produce great amounts of horsepower. It is turbo-charged, which means that a small turbine is attached to the engine. The turbine uses exhaust gases to drive more air and fuel into the combustion chamber. This way, a car with a smaller engine makes the power of one with a bigger engine. That's exactly what the GNX does. There are other changes inside Buick's V-6 to make it durable on the road.

Comfort of a Family Car

Climb into the GNX and you might never know what a monster this car is under the hood. Aside from the jet black paint and extra instruments, this car seems like any Buick Regal. The ride is comfortable and quiet. The stereo tunes in your favorite radio station. But drive to a dragstrip and mash down that accelerator, and you've just released the incredible power of the Buick GNX!

1968 OLDSMOBILE 4-4-2

 **PERFORMANCE:**
Zero to 60 MPH: 6.1 seconds
1/4 Mile Acceleration: 14.1 seconds at 104 MPH
Maximum Speed: 125 MPH

SPECIFICATIONS

⏰ ENGINE:

Type: V-8
Valve Gear: Overhead valves, pushrod operated
Displacement: 400 cubic inches
Compression Ratio: 10.5:1
Horsepower: 360 at 5400 RPM

 CHASSIS:

Body/Frame: Steel body and frame
Wheels: 14 × 8-inch, front and rear
Tires: F70 × 14 front, F70 × 14 rear
Brakes: Front disc, rear drum
Front Suspension: Independent, coil springs
Rear Suspension: Solid axle, leaf springs

Special Series

Like some other muscle cars, the Oldsmobile started out as an option package that gave extra "punch" to a garden-variety sedan. The muscular 4-4-2 began as a Cutlass, with room for the whole family in comfort and style. But in 1968, the 4-4-2 became a separate model from the Cutlass, and the muscle car fan knew exactly what to buy.

Power to Spare

Buying a 4-4-2 was a thrill. Those three numbers meant the high-performance fan got a 400-cubic-inch engine, a four-barrel carburetor, and a dual exhaust system—which added up to 360 horse-power! There was plenty of power to tow a trailer on family vacations, or maybe visit the dragstrip on weekends!

Special Equipment

Besides the muscle motor under the hood, the 4-4-2 came with other special equipment. Heavy-duty suspension pieces balanced out the high-horsepower engine. Larger wheels and tires kept a good grip on the road. And 4-4-2 badges plus a paint stripe let everyone know this car was one mean machine!

Fun in the Sun

Of course, nothing could be better than a convertible muscle car, and the 4-4-2 was one of the
best. Check the right option box and a classic
convertible was yours for the asking. With the electric
top down on a sunny day, the song of the 4-4-2
engine was even more exciting to listen to. It was a
great year for the new car buyer—especially for the
Oldsmobile fan.

1970 PONTIAC FIREBIRD TRANS AM

 **PERFORMANCE:**

Zero to 60 MPH: 6.2 seconds
1/4 Mile Acceleration: 14 seconds at 103 MPH
Maximum Speed: 130 MPH

SPECIFICATIONS

 **ENGINE:**

Type: V-8
Valve Gear: Overhead valves, pushrod operated
Displacement: 400 cubic inches
Compression Ratio: 10.9:1
Horsepower: 345 at 5000 RPM

CHASSIS:

Body/Frame: Steel body and frame
Wheels: 15-inch front, 15-inch rear
Tires: F60 × 15 front, F60 × 15 rear
Brakes: Front disc, rear drum
Front Suspension: Independent, coil springs
Rear Suspension: Solid axle, leaf springs

27

The Camaro's Sister Car

When Chevrolet came out with the first Camaro in 1967, Pontiac was ready to build a sister car called the Firebird. It would be the same car in many ways, but the engineers at Pontiac made some special changes they hoped would make the Firebird a competitive muscle car.

Checking the Option Box

Like other real muscle cars, the Trans Am was really just an option package that built up a "normal" car into a street racer. The right options when buying a Pontiac Firebird would get you the Trans Am package, with several engine choices. In 1970, you could have a 400-cubic-inch V-8 engine with 345 horsepower!

Great Ride, Great Handling

Pontiac's changes to the Camaro design were very helpful. They made the car ride comfortably on the road, but kept it able to corner like a sports car. Disc brakes stop the car from high speed easily. And that big-horsepower engine helps you have fun in straight line or on a twisty road.

On the Road

No other muscle car has had as many fender flares, spoilers, and decals as the Trans Am. These features let others know that you aren't driving just any Firebird. The best part of the Trans Am is how much fun it is to drive. It doesn't have enough horsepower to scare you like a Chrysler Hemi or a Shelby Cobra, but it has enough so that you feel great going through the gears. At the same time, you can flick the tail of the car around, power-steering your way through fast turns, just like a race driver. The Trans Am is an excellent muscle car to own and to drive.

1968 SHELBY MUSTANG GT500

PERFORMANCE:
Zero to 60 MPH: 5.2 seconds
1/4 Mile Acceleration: 13.87 seconds at 102 MPH
Maximum Speed: 140 MPH

SPECIFICATIONS

 **ENGINE:**
Type: V-8
Valve Gear: Overhead valves, pushrod operated
Displacement: 428 cubic inches
Compression Ratio: 10.5:1
Horsepower: 335 at 5200 RPM

CHASSIS:
Body/Frame: Steel body and frame
Wheels: 15 × 7 inches front, 15 × 7 inches rear
Tires: F60-15 front, F60-15 rear
Brakes: Front disc, rear drum
Front Suspension: Independent, coil springs
Rear Suspension: Solid axle, leaf springs

Shelby Power in a Mustang

The start of the "Shelby Mustang" was in 1965 with the GT350. This car was a highly modified 289 Mustang, with different bodywork, engine, and suspension pieces. The Shelby touch had created another street legend. Then in 1967, the latest version of the Mustang got more bodywork modifications and the 428-cubic-inch Cobra engine.

Performance and Handling

The modifications to these limited-edition Shelbys were meant to balance out the handling and braking with muscle car power. The Shelby team added better brakes, lighter wheels, and wider tires. This combination made the GT500 one of the most popular Shelbys ever.

Special Styling

At Shelby, they styled the GT500 so that it was hard to tell there was a Mustang under that body. The front end was made of fiberglass to save weight and give the car a new look. Special decals identified the car as a GT500. Inside, the luxury options such as air conditioning became available, and with all these, sales of the GT500 increased.

Behind the Wheel

It is always exciting to be aboard a limited-edition machine like the GT500. You know that this is no ordinary car. While designing it, the manufacturer took extra care during every step. A car like this makes the driver feel special, too, knowing that many other people wish for a chance to take a ride in one of the most incredible muscle cars of all time — the Shelby GT500!

1970 AMERICAN MOTORS AMX

 **PERFORMANCE:**
Zero to 60 MPH: 6.2 seconds
1/4 Mile Acceleration: 14 seconds at 100 MPH
Maximum Speed: 120 MPH

SPECIFICATIONS

 **ENGINE:**
Type: V-8
Valve Gear: Overhead valves, pushrod operated
Displacement: 390 cubic inches
Compression Ratio: 10.0:1
Horsepower: 325 at 5000 RPM

CHASSIS:
Body/Frame: Steel body and frame
Wheels: 14-inch, front and rear
Tires: E78 × 14, front and rear
Brakes: Front disc, rear drum
Front Suspension: Independent, coil springs
Rear Suspension: Solid axle, lead springs

Into the Horsepower Race

In the 1960s, all of the American automobile companies were involved in the race to have the fastest car on the track and on the street. Ford had its Mustang and Cobra, Chevrolet had its Corvette and Camaro, and Chrysler had the Hemi cars. American Motors entered the race with the Javelin, and later the AMX.

Two-Seater

The AMX was really a modified Javelin, with a shorter length and only two seats. It was meant to be a sports car with V-8 muscle. A new 390-cubic-inch engine produced 325 horsepower, which put the AMX right on the track in the race for the most horsepower.

A Good Performer

For American Motors' first entry into the muscle car category, the Javelin and AMX were very good. They each combined very sporty looks with good handling and power outputs. The AMX came with either a three-speed automatic or a four-speed manual transmission so the buyer could choose how he or she wanted to shift. Zero to 100 MPH was in a very quick 16 seconds!

The Only American Motors Muscle Car

Unfortunately, American Motors entered the horse-power race a little too late. It was a small company that couldn't spend much money to improve its design like the other car companies did, and soon it stopped selling the AMX. The car just wasn't as successful as it should have been.

Behind the Wheel

With the AMX, it was easy to power around turns with the tail hanging out just like on other muscle cars. The 390-cubic-inch V-8 provided plenty of torque. You could muscle this machine down a dragstrip, too, and come up with 14-second quarter-mile times!

1969 PONTIAC GTO

 **PERFORMANCE:**
Zero to 60 MPH: Approximately 5.8 seconds
1/4 Mile Acceleration: 13.08 seconds at 106 MPH
Maximum Speed: 125 MPH

SPECIFICATIONS

 **ENGINE:**
Type: V-8
Valve Gear: Overhead valves, pushrod operated
Displacement: 400 cubic inches
Compression Ratio: 10.75:1
Horsepower: 370 at 5400 RPM

Chassis:
Body/Frame: Steel body and frame
Wheels: 14-inch, front and rear
Tires: F70 × 14 front, F70 × 14 rear
Brakes: Disc front, drum rear
Front Suspension: Independent, coil springs
Rear Suspension: Solid axle, leaf springs

Smaller Car with a Big Engine

Pontiac's GTO was one of its most successful models ever. With eye-catching styling, and plenty of room for five people, the GTO gave America a muscle car that could be a hot rod and a family car at the same time.

The Original Muscle Car

Many people consider the GTO as the first true muscle car. Stuffing a big engine into a family car was nothing new, but when General Motors got into the act, it was good news for horsepower lovers. With nicknames like "the judge" and "goat," it's easy to see how loyal owners of this Pontiac can be!

Styling Changes

The original GTO had a steel front end, but in later years a cleaner-looking plastic front section was created. Right on the radiator was a "GTO" emblem, showing other drivers this car was not to be messed with. There was also a convertible available, which helped make cruising so popular—everyone could see who the lucky driver was!

Not a New Car

Almost like the Camaro Z-28 of the 1960s, the GTO began as just an option package selected by the owner of a Pontiac Le Mans. In fact, at first the car was called the Le Mans GTO. After a few years of production, the GTO became a separate perform-ance model from Pontiac.

"Ram Air V-8"

The huge 400-cubic-inch V-8 engine in the GTO makes the car the muscle car it is. Functional hood scoops and standard dual exhaust let the engine breathe easy. By checking the right option box, you could have a "Ram Air IV" monster motor with 370 horsepower!

41

1970 DODGE CHALLENGER R/T

 **PERFORMANCE:**
Zero to 60 MPH: 5.6 seconds
1/4 Mile Acceleration: 14 seconds at 104 MPH
Maximum Speed: 135 MPH

SPECIFICATIONS

 **ENGINE:**
Type: V-8
Valve Gear: Overhead valves, pushrod operated
Displacement: 426 cubic inches
Compression Ratio: 10.25:1
Horsepower: 425 at 5000 RPM

CHASSIS:
Body/Frame: Steel body and frame
Wheels: 14-inch, front and rear
Tires: F70 × 14, front and rear
Brakes: Front disc, rear drum
Front Suspension: Independent, torsion bar
Rear Suspension: Solid axle, leaf springs

"Hemi" Engine

If you went to a Dodge dealer in 1970 and checked the right option boxes on a brand-new Charger, you could have ended up with one of the meanest, quickest muscle cars around. The 383-cubic-inch engine was standard, putting out 335 horsepower. Checking the option boxes could give you a 440 "six-pack" engine with 375 horses or even the legendary 426 "Hemi" with 430 horsepower!

Modified Suspension

The Challenger was an all-new model in 1970 and was lower and shorter than any other Dodge at the time. It made perfect sense to slip in any of Dodge's powerhouse engines and build up one of the best muscle cars around! Naturally the Challenger had to have a stiffer suspension and better brakes than past Dodge models, and this helped the car to have good handling at high speeds.

A Convertible Option

Like many other muscle cars, the Challenger was available as a convertible. It may be one of the best-looking convertibles ever put together. Its lines still look modern, even today. It's no wonder that these cars are worth more and more money each year!

"Scat Pack"

"Scat Pack" is a name that Dodge gave to a group of its fastest cars. The Challenger is one of the famous members of this special group of machines. Whatever engine option you chose with the Challenger R/T, your membership in the "Scat Pack" was certain!

Behind the Wheel

Nothing can match the thrill of sitting in the driver's seat of a car with a huge V-8 engine under the hood. With a car as nice to look at as the Challenger, you can't go wrong. Start the engine and just sit back and listen. You are hearing a sound that will never be heard from a new car again—the sound of a big-block Dodge V-8, from the scat pack!

1967 CHEVROLET CORVETTE

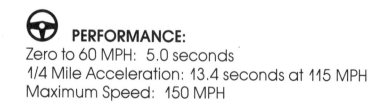 **PERFORMANCE:**
Zero to 60 MPH: 5.0 seconds
1/4 Mile Acceleration: 13.4 seconds at 115 MPH
Maximum Speed: 150 MPH

SPECIFICATIONS

 **ENGINE:**
Type: V-8
Valve Gear: Overhead valves, pushrod operated
Displacement: 427 cubic inches
Compression Ratio: 11:1
Horsepower: 435 at 6400 RPM

CHASSIS:
Body/Frame: Fiberglass body on steel frame
Wheels: 15-inch, front and rear
Tires: F70 × 15 inches, front and rear
Brakes: Front and rear discs
Front Suspension: Independent
Rear Suspension: Independent, leaf spring

America's Favorite

No car means American muscle like the Chevy Corvette. It has been around for more than thirty years, getting better and better all the time, with V-8 power that is legendary. From its beginnings as a slow six-cylinder in 1953 to its fire-breathing V-8 engine of the 1960s, the Corvette has always been America's favorite muscle car.

Fastest on the Block

Almost always, if there was a Corvette parked on your street, you knew it had to be the fastest, best-looking car in the neighborhood. In 1967 your Corvette could have the 427-cubic-inch engine with 435 horsepower! There was not much on the road that could touch a Corvette, for performance or style.

Fiberglass Body

The special fiberglass body of the Corvette allowed it to be shaped with many curves and cutouts. The fins on the side of the Corvette have almost always been there, and they help make the car look mus-cular and mean, almost like a shark. The fiberglass body is also lighter than metal, which helps the Corvette thunder down the road even faster.

On the Road in the Corvette

Inside the 1967 model, it is a little cramped. There is not much room in the cockpit because the engine takes up most of the room in the car! Fire up the V-8 and it burbles loudly. The best Corvette to drive is the convertible, because you can let the sun shine on your head and the wind rush through your hair. All that combined with one of the all-time greatest muscle cars makes you want to keep driving forever!

1968 MERCURY COUGAR XR-7

 **PERFORMANCE:**
Zero to 60 MPH: 6.1 seconds
1/4 Mile Acceleration: 14.2 seconds at 102 MPH
Maximum Speed: 125 MPH

SPECIFICATIONS

 **ENGINE:**

Type: V-8
Valve Gear: Overhead valves, pushrod operated
Displacement: 428 cubic inches
Compression Ratio: 10.5:1
Horsepower: 335 at 4600 RPM

CHASSIS:

Body/Frame: Steel body and frame
Wheels: 14-inch, front and rear
Tires: 7.35 × 14-inch, front and rear
Brakes: Front disc, rear drum
Front Suspension: Independent
Rear Suspension: Solid axle, leaf springs

A Mustang's Closest Relative

The Mercury Cougar was one of the less popular muscle cars of the 1960s. This isn't because it wasn't a good car—it is the same car as the Ford Mustang under the skin. But people who wanted a muscle car liked the sportier looks of the Mustang. For Mercury fans, the slightly larger Cougar offered a nice alternative muscle car to the Ford Mustang.

Smooth Styling

Many people think the Cougar was a better-looking car than the Mustang. It is styled smoothly, with hidden headlights and a longer body. The engines offered were the same, but the Cougar already came with the 289-cubic-inch V-8, which was an extra-cost option in the Mustang.

Luxury Muscle Car

The Cougar also had many more comfort features and gadgets than the Mustang. Again, by checking the right option box, you could have your choice of a CB radio, leather seats, or even a ski carrier! The Cougar also had a slightly softer suspension than the Mustang, for a more comfortable ride.

428 V-8

If you were to order the Cougar GT-E package, you
would get the famous 428-cubic-inch V-8 with 335
horsepower. You would also get a stiffer suspension,
wider wheels and tires, and better brakes. Hood
scoops and a special exhaust system completed
the package. The Cougar GT-E was just one of many
special versions of the Cougar you could buy.

Behind the Wheel

Inside the Cougar, it is nice and comfortable. You can't
really tell that there is a huge V-8 under the hood.
But when you start the engine, your foot realizes that
it can unleash muscle-car power by pushing down on
the throttle. Nail the throttle and you take off in a
cloud of burnt rubber, looking for the highway ahead.

53

1967 PLYMOUTH BELVEDERE GTX

 **PERFORMANCE:**
Zero to 60 MPH: 5.4 seconds
1/4 Mile Acceleration: 14 seconds at 97 MPH
Maximum Speed: 140 MPH

54

SPECIFICATIONS

 **ENGINE:**

Type: V-8
Valve Gear: Overhead valves, pushrod operated
Displacement: 426 cubic inches
Compression Ratio: 10.25:1
Horsepower: 425 at 5000 RPM

CHASSIS:

Body/Frame: Steel body and frame
Wheels: 14-inch, front and rear
Tires: 7.75 × 14 front, 7.75 × 14 rear
Brakes: Front disc, rear drum
Front Suspension: Independent, torsion bars
Rear Suspension: Solid axle, leaf springs

The Family Muscle Car

The Belvedere model from Plymouth was another family sedan that could become a fire-breathing muscle car if you ordered the right options. In this case, the six-person Belvedere could be had with any of Plymouth's high-performance engines, from the 440 to the 426 Hemi. Try to imagine you and your family driving around in a 426 Hemi muscle car!

Heavy-Duty Suspension

Like most of the big-engined Plymouths, the Belvedere has a much stiffer suspension than the smaller-engined cars. This change is very important, because with the power of that engine the heavy weight of the Belvedere might get out of control. That wouldn't be good in a family car! So Plymouth engineered a heavy-duty suspension system to keep the car balanced.

Under the Hood

Pop the hood of the Belvedere and gaze at the engine. Its awesome horsepower is right in front of you. The engine bay is huge, but the Hemi almost fills it up. A chrome air cleaner hides the two carburetors. All the parts are there, tempting you to get in and start the engine. But just looking at the Hemi engine is fun enough, for now!

Driving the Belvedere

One thing you notice about the Belvedere, whether it is a hardtop or convertible, is how much room there is inside. It seems as big as some people's living rooms! The instrument panel is simple but useful to look at. And driving on the road gives you the thrill of having that Hemi V-8 just waiting to rocket you up to light speed!

1970 PLYMOUTH ROAD RUNNER SUPERBIR

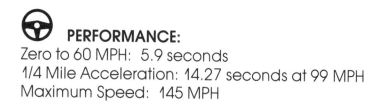 **PERFORMANCE:**
Zero to 60 MPH: 5.9 seconds
1/4 Mile Acceleration: 14.27 seconds at 99 MPH
Maximum Speed: 145 MPH

SPECIFICATIONS

 **ENGINE:**

Type: V-8
Valve Gear: Overhead valves, pushrod operated
Displacement: 440 cubic inches
Compression Ratio: 10.1:1
Horsepower: 375 at 4600 RPM

CHASSIS:

Body/Frame: Steel body and frame
Wheels: 14-inch front, 14-inch rear
Tires: F70 × 14 front, F70 × 14 rear
Brakes: Front disc, rear drum
Front Suspension: Independent
Rear Suspension: Solid axle, leaf springs

The Most Awesome-Looking Muscle Car Ever

Nothing can prepare you for the sight of a Superbird. You probably haven't seen one on the street, and you probably won't. It was a car that Plymouth built only because they had to. The rules of racing said that Plymouth had to build a certain number of cars that looked *exactly* like the cars that were going to race. The Superbird is that car.

Race Car Styling

The front and rear ends of the Superbird are what people notice the most. The front of the car has a large plastic cap on it, containing the headlights. It is rounded in shape so that it can slice through the wind better. The rear end of the Superbird has a huge ''wing'' sticking out from the body. This helps keep the rear end of the car down on the ground at high speeds.

From the Track to the Street

Plymouth built cars like the Superbird to compete against other car companies at racetracks all over the country. In the 1970s, companies had to build race cars that looked exactly the same as street cars. So, Plymouth decided to build a race car for the street! That way, Plymouth would win on the track and on the streets.

"Beep Beep" Goes the Horn

The horn of the Road Runner Superbird makes the same sound as the cartoon character it is named after—"Beep Beep!" If you look closely, there is even a sticker on both the front and rear ends of the Road Runner! In the same way that Wile E. Coyote can never catch the cartoon Road Runner, no other car can catch the Superbird!

GLOSSARY

Accelerator—A pedal on the floor of the car (also known as the gas pedal) that is connected by a cable to a valve inside the carburetor. Pushing down on the accelerator opens the valve, increasing engine speed.

Anti-lock Brakes—Computer-controlled braking system that allows for quick, safe stops in any condition.

Body—The external sheet metal of the vehicle.

Carburetor—A hollow metal block with a valve that opens and closes, controlling the amount of air and fuel pumped into the engine.

Combustion Chamber—A chamber above the piston, containing the spark plug and valves. When the valves let in fuel and air, the spark plug ignites the mixture and an explosion occurs, forcing the piston to move.

Compression Ratio—The ratio of how tightly the piston compresses the air in the combustion chamber to the volume of the cylinder.

Cylinder—A round, hollow tube inside the engine, in which the piston moves up and down.

Disc Brake—A flat, round disc that is gripped by a caliper when the brakes are applied, slowing down the car.

Displacement—The size of the engine, which depends on the size of the pistons.

Drum Brake—A round "drum" connected to the wheel. Inside the drum are "shoes" that push against the drum when the brake is applied, slowing down the car.

Fender Flares—Extra bodywork that widens the car's fenders, allowing larger wheels and tires to be used.

Fiberglass—A very light, strong material made of tiny glass fibers. Fiberglass is used to make the body of the Corvette.

Frame—A structure of welded metal bars underneath a car that attaches the body to the suspension.

Front Suspension—A series of linkages, springs, and shock absorbers that controls the action of the steering wheel and front of the car on the road.

"Hemi" Engine—A very high performance, limited-production engine in some Dodge and Plymouth automobiles. The "Hemi" name comes from the hemispherical shape of the combustion chambers inside the engine.

Horsepower—A measurement of how much power the engine can put out.

Intake Manifold—A set of metal tubes that guides the air and fuel mixture into the engine from the carburetor.

Limited Edition—A car that is made in very few numbers, such as the Buick GNX.

Manifold—See intake manifold.

Options—The extra-cost parts that can be ordered when buying a new car. Examples are a larger engine, special wheels and tires, or air conditioning. Options let the buyer "customize" a car the way he or she wants it to be.

Piston—A circular piece of metal that is moved up and down inside the cylinder by an explosion in the combustion chamber.

Pushrod—A thin rod that pushes against a lever called the "rocker arm," opening a valve in the combustion chamber.

Quadra Shock—A rear suspension with four shock absorbers, used on new Ford cars such as the Mustang GT.

1/4 Mile Acceleration—The time it takes for a car to go from standing still to one-quarter of a mile away, and the speed it has reached when it gets there.

Radiator—A metal block of tiny fins that capture cool air. The cool air is transferred to the hot water/antifreeze mixture from inside the engine. The radiator lowers temperature of the water/antifreeze mixture used to cool the inside of the engine.

Rear Suspension—A series of linkages, springs, and shock absorbers that controls the action of the rear of the car on the road.

Scat Pack—A nickname given to the high-performance muscle cars from Plymouth.

Shelby—A special, high-performance type of car built by a man named Carroll Shelby.

"Six Pack"—The nickname for a set of three high-performance two-barrel carburetors in some Dodge and Plymouth automobiles.

Spoilers—Special "fins" attached to the front or rear of the car that "spoil" the effect of the wind, helping to keep the car more stable.

Torque—The effort needed inside the engine to turn the rear wheels of the car. The bigger the explosion in the combustion chamber, the more torque.

Turbocharger—A small turbine that is spun at very high speeds by exhaust gases. The turbocharger forces extra air and fuel into an engine, allowing a smaller engine to have as much horsepower as some larger engines.

Valve—A mushroom-shaped piece of metal that lets the air/fuel mixture into the combustion chamber, while another valve lets out burnt exhaust gases.

Valve Gear—The type of system an engine uses to open and close valves.

V-8 Engine—An eight-cylinder engine in which all of its cylinders line up in the shape of a "V."

Zero to 60 Miles per Hour—The time it takes for a car to go from standing still to a speed of 60 miles per hour.

INDEX